P9-BYU-663

THE MIGHTY ATLANTIC OCEAN

Doreen Gonzales

Enslow Elementary
an imprint of
Enslow Publishers, Inc.
40 Industrial Road
Box 398
Berkeley Heights, NJ 07922
USA

http://www.enslow.com

Enslow Elementary, an imprint of Enslow Publishers, Inc.

Enslow Elementary is a registered trademark of Enslow Publishers, Inc.

Library of Congress Cataloging-in-Publication Data:
Gonzales, Doreen.
    The mighty Atlantic ocean / Doreen Gonzales.
      p. cm. — (Our earth's oceans)
    Includes index.
    Summary: "Learn about the Atlantic Ocean, the animals that call it home, and the seafloor. Also read about the
people who have explored it and what is being done to keep the Atlantic clean"—Provided by publisher.
    ISBN 978-0-7660-4088-5
    1. Atlantic Ocean—Juvenile literature. I. Title.
    GC481.G66 2013
    551.46'13—dc23
                   2012007615

Future editions:
Paperback ISBN 978-1-4644-0152-7
ePUB ISBN 978-1-4645-1059-5
Single User PDF ISBN 978-1-4646-1059-2
Multi-User PDF ISBN 978-0-7660-4437-1

Printed in the United States of America
102012 Lake Book Manufacturing, Inc., Melrose Park, IL

10 9 8 7 6 5 4 3 2 1

To Our Readers: We have done our best to make sure all Internet Addresses in this book were active and appropriate when we went to press. However, the author and the publisher have no control over and assume no liability for the material available on those Internet sites or on other Web sites they may link to. Any comments or suggestions can be sent by e-mail to comments@enslow.com or to the address on the back cover.

♻ Enslow Publishers, Inc., is committed to printing our books on recycled paper. The paper in every book contains 10% to 30% post-consumer waste (PCW). The cover board on the outside of each book contains 100% PCW. Our goal is to do our part to help young people and the environment too!

Photo Credits: © C Wylie Misselhorn, p. 13; Commander John Bortniak, National Oceanic and Atmospheric Administration (NOAA), p. 42; © Corel Corporation, pp. 12, 26, 27, 28; Environmental Protection Agency, p. 40; © GeoAtlas, p. 4; Image courtesy of H. Scott Meister, SCDNR, p. 30; © Library of Congress, p. 32; National Marine Fisheries Service, pp. 24, 35; NOAA, p. 17; © 2011 Photos.com, a division of Getty Images. All rights reserved., p. 29; © 2011 Photos.com, a division of Getty Images. All rights reserved.: Eddie Thomas, pp. 8–9, Franck Camhi, p. 37, Martin Jakobsson, p. 20, Nancy Nehring, p. 14, Ragnar Larusson, p. 22, Rüdiger Baun, p. 10 (left) Vlad Ghiea, p. 10 (right); Shutterstock.com, pp. 3, 5, 7, 11, 16, 23, 31, 36, 38, 39, 44, running heads; This image comes from The Report of the Scientific Results of the Exploring Voyage of H.M.S. *Challenger* during the years 1873-1876 published 1885-95., p. 34; © Tom LaBaff, p. 15; USGS, pp. 18, 21; Wikipedia, p. 33.

Cover Credit: Jupiterimages/Photos.com (bottom right); Shutterstock.com (top right, top left, bottom left)

Table of
CONTENTS

The Mighty Atlantic Ocean

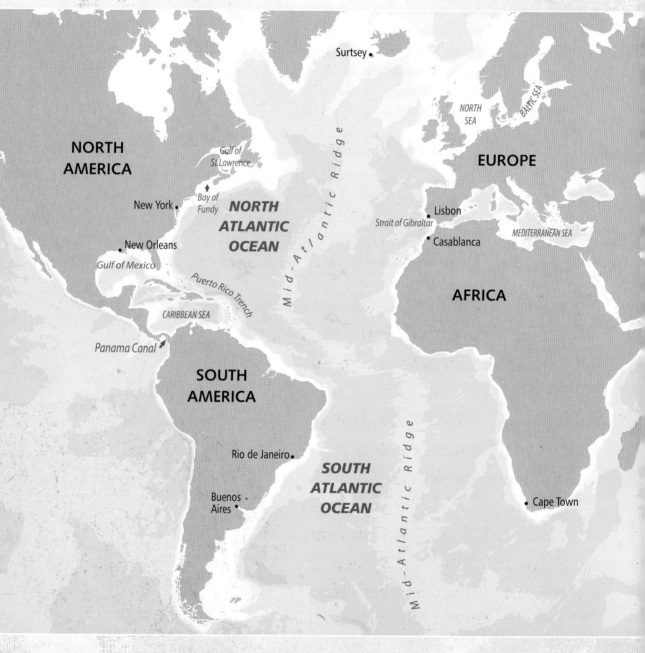

Surtsey

NORTH SEA

BALTIC SEA

NORTH AMERICA

EUROPE

Gulf of St.Lawrence

New York

Bay of Fundy

NORTH ATLANTIC OCEAN

Mid-Atlantic Ridge

Lisbon

Strait of Gibraltar

MEDITERRANEAN SEA

New Orleans

Casablanca

Gulf of Mexico

AFRICA

Puerto Rico Trench

CARIBBEAN SEA

Panama Canal

SOUTH AMERICA

SOUTH ATLANTIC OCEAN

Mid-Atlantic Ridge

Rio de Janeiro

Buenos Aires

Cape Town

Chapter 1

The MIGHTY ATLANTIC

The Atlantic Ocean is the world's second largest ocean. Only the Pacific Ocean is larger. From the shores of North America to the coast of Africa, the mighty Atlantic Ocean covers over 29 million square miles (76 million square kilometers). That's about a fifth of Earth's surface.

North and South America form the Atlantic's western boundary. Europe and Africa are its eastern

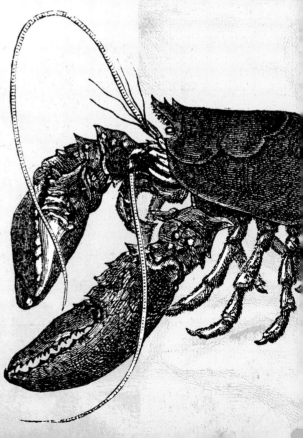

boundary. The Atlantic Ocean borders the Arctic Ocean in the north. In the south, it meets the Southern Ocean.

The Atlantic is 5,500 miles (8,850 kilometers) across at its widest point. It is about two times as long as it is wide. The average depth of the Atlantic Ocean is 12,800 feet (3,926 meters).

Climate

The temperature of the surface water near the equator is about 86°F (30°C). The temperature drops as the water gets deeper. Water at the bottom of the ocean is just above freezing.

Water also gets colder the farther it is from the equator. Some Atlantic waters get cold enough to freeze. The Baltic Sea, for example, is frozen from October to June.

Currents

There are many currents in the Atlantic. A current is like a river in the sea. It moves water in a constant and regular course. Currents in the South Atlantic move counterclockwise.

Currents in the North Atlantic move clockwise. The strongest North Atlantic current is the Gulf Stream. It begins near the equator and moves northward along the east coast of the United States. The Gulf Stream then flows toward northwestern Europe.

Warm waters from the Gulf Stream keep parts of the North Atlantic from freezing. The waters also release their heat into the air. This warms the nearby land.

Waves from the Atlantic Ocean break on a North Carolina beach.

Tides

Atlantic waters move with tides, too. Tides are
caused by the moon's gravity. When the moon is
on one side of an ocean, its gravity pulls the water
toward it. This pulls waves farther and farther
onto the shore.

As the earth and moon move, the moon
begins pulling on different waters. Now these

waters move higher onto the shore. Water that was rising begins to fall back.

When water reaches its highest point on shore, it is said to be at high tide. Water is at low tide when it has fallen back to its lowest point. Most seacoasts have two high tides and two low tides each day. In the Atlantic, Canada's Bay of Fundy has the greatest difference between high and low tides.

In the Atlantic at Canada's Bay of Fundy, the difference between low tide (left) and high tide (right) can be as much as 53 feet (16 meters).

Winds

Ocean winds cause waves. Winds can also create cyclones and hurricanes. These are storms with winds that whirl around and around. Most form near the equator.

Hurricane winds can blow faster than 100 miles (160 kilometers) per hour. Winds this strong can capsize ships and set off huge waves that flood nearby coasts. Sometimes hurricanes move onto land. They can cause floods, destruction, and death.

Chapter 2

Resources from
THE SEA

The Atlantic Ocean is rich in resources. Many are used to make things that people use every day.

Fish and Marine Life

Lots of seafood comes from the Atlantic Ocean. Some of it is raised on fish farms along the coast. Some of it is caught by people in small boats. However, most of the fish that comes from the Atlantic Ocean is caught by people on huge

fishing ships. These ships use large nets that bring up thousands of fish at once. The fish are cleaned, packaged, and frozen right on the ship.

Certain parts of the Atlantic Ocean have lots of fish. These areas are called fisheries. The Atlantic has some of the best fisheries in the world. One of the largest is in the North Sea.

Energy

The Atlantic also supplies the world with oil and natural gas. These resources lie below the seabed. Offshore oil rigs are built over the ocean to drill down and pump them to the surface. These rigs are often huge. Some even have sleeping quarters so that workers can stay there for days.

Ocean tides are also used to make electricity. One large power plant in France uses the motion of the water to make electricity.

A fisherman pulls in cod from the Atlantic off the coast of Nova Scotia, Canada. This area is one of the Atlantic Ocean's largest fisheries, especially for cod.

Salt and Sand

Salt is another resource that comes from the Atlantic. It is removed by heating large pools of ocean water. When the water evaporates, the salt is left behind.

Sand and gravel are also taken from the Atlantic Ocean. They are used in construction and for making concrete.

Medicine

Some medicines can be made from marine animals. One important medicine called cytarabine is made from a sponge that lives in the Caribbean Sea. Cytarabine is used to treat an illness called lymphoma.

The cancer-fighting drug cytarabine is made from a sponge that lives in the Caribbean Sea.

Transportation

The Atlantic is one of the world's busiest oceans. Ships filled with cargo and passengers cross it every day.

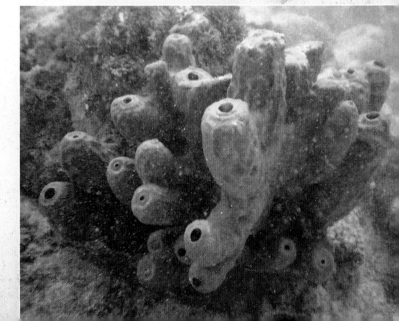

The Atlantic Ocean contains several seas that are reached by sailing through small passageways. For example, the Strait of Gibraltar connects the Atlantic Ocean to the Mediterranean Sea.

The Panama Canal is a man-made shortcut through the country of Panama. It links the Atlantic Ocean to the Pacific Ocean.

Instead of traveling around South America, a ship traveling from New York to San Francisco can pass through the 50-mile (80-kilometer) Panama Canal, taking 7,872 miles (12,669 kilometers) off the trip!

Water Cycle

Perhaps the most important role of the Atlantic is its vital part in the water cycle. Ocean water evaporates into the air. The vapor condenses, then falls as rain or snow. Much of this precipitation falls directly into the ocean. Some falls on land and is used by plants, animals, and people. Unused precipitation flows into rivers and runs back to the sea. There the cycle begins again.

The oceans are a vital part of the earth's water cycle.

clouds where water condenses

sun

rain

EVAPORATION

OCEAN

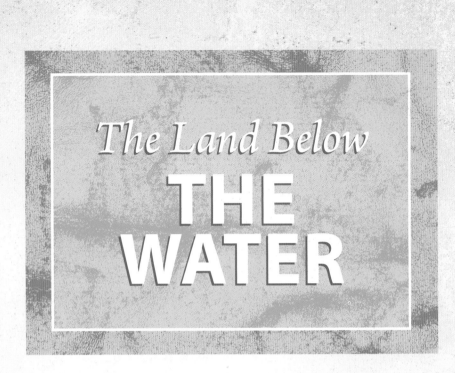

The Land Below
THE WATER

The floor of the Atlantic Ocean is not flat. It contains a variety of land formations.

Continental Shelf

The bottom of the Atlantic Ocean slopes gently as it moves away from land. This incline is called a continental shelf. In some places, the Atlantic's continental shelf extends 300 miles (480 kilometers) from the shore. In other places, it is only 100 miles (160 kilometers) wide.

The seafloor drops sharply at the end of the continental shelf. At the bottom is the bed of the deep sea. This is called the abyss.

Abyssal Plains

Much of the Atlantic abyss is flat. These large flat areas are known as abyssal plains. The Atlantic Ocean has many abyssal plains. The largest is the Canary Abyssal Plain. It is west of the Canary Islands. It covers an area of 350,000 square miles (900,000 square kilometers).

Many animals, including this blackbellied rosefish and rock crab, are found along the ocean floor off the coast of New Jersey.

Trenches

A few narrow valleys cut through the Atlantic abyss. These are called trenches. The Atlantic's longest trench is the Puerto Rico Trench. The deepest place in the Atlantic is in this trench.

The islands in the Caribbean Sea are actually the tops of mountains in a long, submerged chain.

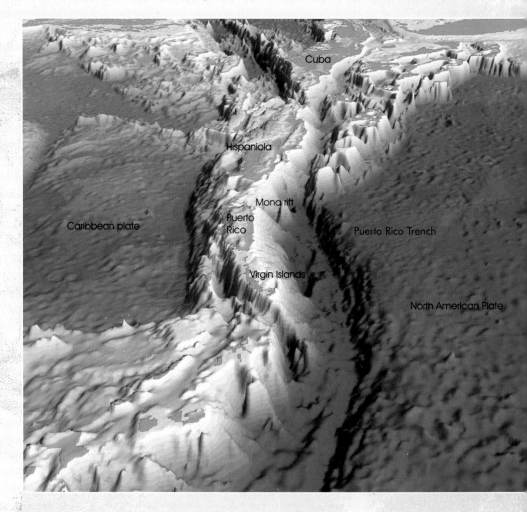

It is called the Milwaukee Deep. The bottom of the Milwaukee Deep is 30,246 feet (9,219 meters) below the ocean's surface.

Mountains

There are mountains on the bottom of the Atlantic Ocean, too. One range is called the Mid-Atlantic Ridge.

Most mountains in the Mid-Atlantic Ridge lie far below the ocean's surface. In a few places, though, peaks break through the water. These peaks are islands. The Azores islands, for example, are mountaintops in the Mid-Atlantic Ridge.

The Mid-Atlantic Ridge is part of a longer mountain range called the mid-ocean ridge. This ridge runs through all of the earth's oceans along the edges of tectonic plates. A tectonic plate is a huge piece of rock. Scientists believe the earth's surface sits on thirty different tectonic plates.

The Mid-Atlantic Ridge sits on two plates that are being pulled apart by forces inside the earth. The pulling creates cracks between the plates.

Magma from inside the earth rises, filling the cracks. The cool ocean water hardens the magma and turns it into rock. The rock is now new seafloor. This process is called seafloor spreading.

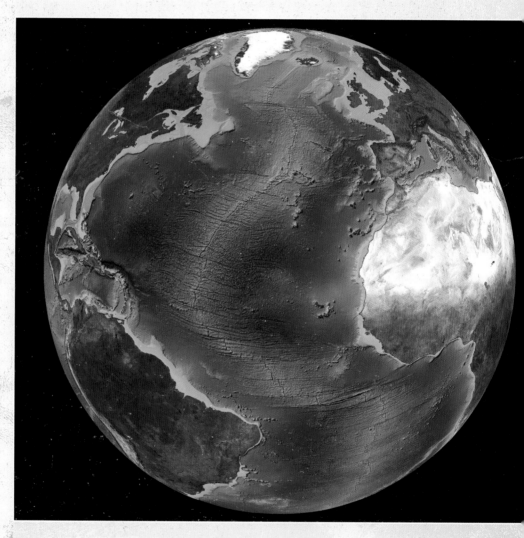

The roughly C-shaped Mid-Atlantic Ridge shows up light blue in the middle of the darker ocean depths.

Major Plate Boundaries

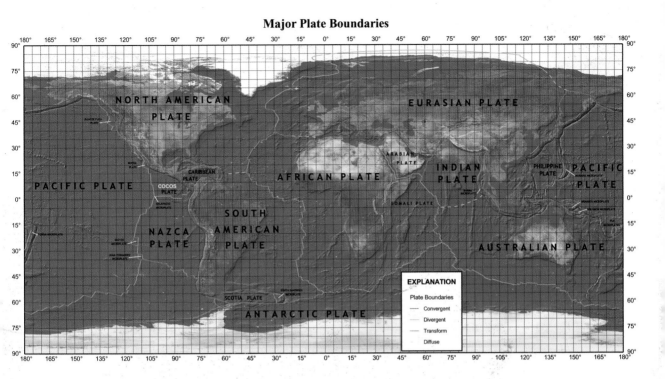

The Mid-Atlantic Ridge spreads about an inch each year. North and South America are slowly moving away from Europe and Africa.

Volcanoes and Earthquakes

Occasionally, there is a volcano or earthquake below the Atlantic. Most occur along the Mid-Atlantic Ridge.

In 1963, a volcano in the North Atlantic erupted until its lava broke the surface of the sea.

The mid-ocean ridge plays an important part in a theory called plate tectonics. According to this theory, the earth's surface sits on thirty huge pieces of rock. These rocks are called plates.

When the lava cooled, a new island was born. The island was named Surtsey. Surtsey is near Iceland.

The floor of the ocean can be a busy place. Forces not seen from above are almost always at work there, changing the shape of the earth.

Surtsey is a volcanic island off the south coast of Iceland. It was created in a volcanic eruption that reached the ocean's surface on November 14, 1963, and lasted until June 5, 1967.

The Atlantic
ECOSYSTEM

Plants and animals are found from the surface of the Atlantic Ocean to its deepest bottom. This life is divided into three groups.

Plankton

The first group is known as plankton. Plankton is made of plants and animals that cannot swim. They drift with the ocean's waves and currents. Many marine animals feed on plankton.

Plants that are plankton are called phytoplankton. Most phytoplankton is so tiny it can only be seen with a microscope. Yet seaweed that floats on the ocean's surface is also phytoplankton. It can grow to be two hundred feet (sixty meters) long.

Zooplankton are animals in the plankton. Most are tiny crustaceans. Crustaceans are animals with jointed legs and hard shells. The most abundant Atlantic zooplankton are copepods and krill.

One of the many kinds of zooplankton that live in the Atlantic Ocean is this ctenophore.

Other zooplankton, such as jellyfish, can be quite large. One Atlantic jellyfish grows tentacles one hundred feet (thirty meters) long.

Nekton

The second group of ocean life is called the nekton. The nekton is made up of animals that swim on their own. Most stay close to the coast. This is where they find the most food.

One group of nekton is animals with backbones, or vertebrates. These include fish, mammals, and reptiles.

Thousands of different kinds of fish live in the Atlantic. Some are small, like the Atlantic herring. It is less than one foot (thirty centimeters) long. Others, like the blue marlin and the sawfish, can be more than ten feet (three meters) in length.

There are more than 350 different kinds of shark in the Atlantic nekton. They can be 8 inches (20 centimeters) to 50 feet (15 meters) long.

Mammals, such as whales, are also part of the nekton. Almost every kind of whale lives in the Atlantic. The smallest are dolphins and porpoises.

The largest are blue whales. Blue whales are also the largest animals on Earth. They grow to 100 feet (30 meters) long and can weigh 200 tons (181 metric tons).

Invertebrates also live in the nekton. These animals do not have a backbone and include squid and octopuses. Octopuses have eight arms. When one is cut off, a new one grows back.

Squid have ten arms. They capture prey with sucking disks on their arms. Squid are able to change the color and patterns on their bodies. Most squid are less than one foot (30 centimeters) long. The giant squid, however, grows to 40 feet (12 meters) long.

Manatees are also part of the Atlantic nekton. It is believed that early explorers, pirates, and sailors may have mistaken colonies of manatees swimming in the Atlantic Ocean for mermaids!

The Atlantic Oval Squid is one of the invertebrates that lives in the nekton. It is able to change its body colors. This may be a way of communicating with others of the same species.

Benthos

The benthos is the last group of life in the ocean. It is found on the sea bottom.

Tide pools are a part of the benthos. These are made when rising and falling tides fill shallow depressions in rocks along the shore. Tide pools often are full of barnacles, urchins, starfish, and other plants and animals.

Farther out to sea, crabs and lobsters live on the ocean floor. In addition, plants such as kelp root themselves to the sea bottom.

A snorkeler takes a look at the coral reefs of Bonaire.

The water in the deepest part of the ocean is cold and dark. Yet even there, life abounds. Some of the strangest-looking animals in all of the sea live here. Many have special organs that give off light so that they can find food.

Polyps and Coral

Another animal of the benthos is the polyp. Polyps live in warm water. They take calcium out of seawater and use it to build their skeletons.

Coral is not just something pretty to look at. It serves a number of purposes, including providing a habitat to many species, filtering water to keep it clean, and preventing erosion to surrounding islands.

Polyps are only an inch long, but they attach to each other like Lego® building blocks.

When a polyp dies, its body decays and the skeleton remains. The skeleton is called coral. Little by little, dead polyps grow into huge coral structures. Coral can grow so big it creates an underwater ridge. This is called a coral reef.

The berry-like structures of sargassum are filled with gas. These structures are called pneumatocysts. They help the plant float.

The Chain of Life

Each group of life is important to the health of the entire ocean ecosystem. Animals in the nekton eat plankton. They become the food for larger nektonic animals. When uneaten animals die, their bodies sink and are eaten by creatures of the benthos. Whatever is not eaten decays into minerals that are carried back to the surface by currents. These minerals become food for the plankton. When any one life-form in this chain is harmed, the life-forms that need it are also harmed. Therefore, each species must stay healthy so that life in the Atlantic Ocean can thrive.

Exploring the
ATLANTIC

The early Romans named the Atlantic Ocean after the Atlas Mountains in Africa. However, they knew very little about its waters.

The First Explorers

The first people to sail the Atlantic Ocean lived at the eastern end of the Mediterranean Sea. They took goods across the Mediterranean as early as 1100 B.C. As time passed, they went farther and farther west.

These early sailors used the stars and sun to navigate. In about 200 B.C., a system of lines was

developed for mapping the ocean. These lines, called latitude and longitude, are still used today.

European Exploration

Viking sailors from Norway began venturing onto the North Atlantic during the A.D 800s. In time, they traveled to Iceland, Greenland, and northern North America.

By the mid-1400s, European sailors began looking for a sea route to Asia. This would make trading with people there easier and cheaper.

One sailor named Christopher Columbus planned to get to Asia by sailing westward across the Atlantic. He set out in 1492. A few months later, he reached islands in the Caribbean Sea.

The painting *Columbus Taking Possession of the New Country* shows Christopher Columbus's arrival at San Salvador. This island in the Caribbean Sea is believed to be where this explorer for Spain first landed.

Columbus thought he was near the coast of Asia. Later explorers realized he had landed near a continent they had not known existed. It came to be known as America. Other expeditions of exploration followed. By 1600, explorers from Europe had sailed most of the Atlantic.

Oceanography

In 1872, a ship named the H.M.S. *Challenger* left England on an oceanographic mission. Oceanography is the study of the ocean. *Challenger* scientists studied water samples from

In the painting *Guest from Overseas*, by Nicholas Roerich, a knarr, or oceangoing cargo vessel, is depicted. Vikings, who were from southern Scandinavia, braved the extreme weather to settle both Greenland and Iceland.

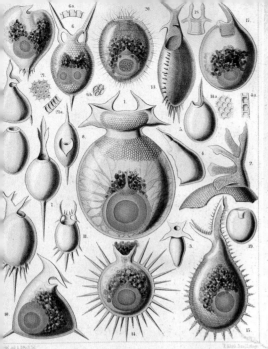

1-15. CHALLENGERIA. 16-18. PHARYNGELLA. 19, 20. ENTOCANNULA.

These drawings show some of the exotic forms of radiolaria collected by H.M.S. *Challenger*. Radiolaria are zooplankton. Their skeletal remains cover large parts of the ocean bottom as radiolarian ooze.

many places in the Atlantic. They found thousands of animals and plants they had never seen before.

During the 1960s, 1970s, and 1980s, scientists studied the earth below the seabed. They learned that the oldest seafloor was near the shores. The newest bed was near the ocean's center. This showed that the seafloor was spreading.

Exploration Today

Today some oceanographers study the ocean in crafts called submersibles. These are small submarines with built-in research equipment. Others study the water from information gathered by satellites high above the earth.

Oceanographers still use research ships, too. Modern ships are like floating laboratories equipped with the latest tools and technology.

There are also laboratories on land devoted to ocean study. One of the most famous is the Woods Hole Oceanographic Institution. It is located on Cape Cod, Massachusetts.

In operation since 1964, *Alvin* was the first deep-sea submersible to be able to carry passengers. At that time, it dove no farther than 35 feet (10 meters). Now the vessel can reach depths of up to 14,764 feet (4,500 meters).

Scientists continue to discover new animals in the Atlantic. They know there are more life-forms to be discovered and more ocean processes to understand.

Keeping the ATLANTIC ALIVE

The Atlantic Ocean is important to everyone. People rely on it for their work, their food, and even for vacations. Yet humans do not always take care of it.

Pollution

Some of the Atlantic is polluted with sewage. Sometimes sewage is dumped right into the ocean. Other times it is released into rivers that run to the sea.

Sewage kills marine life. It can spread disease to people, too.

Chemicals from factories also pollute the Atlantic. Some chemicals kill fish. Others reduce the amount of oxygen in the water. This can kill marine life. People and animals that eat fish that have eaten harmful chemicals can become sick.

Oil is another common pollutant. It can come from spills on land that flow to rivers that flow to

The Atlantic Ocean is not just a place to fish or a method of transportation. It is also a place for people to swim, snorkel, play, and simply relax.

the sea. At times, offshore rigs and oil tankers leak oil into the ocean.

Oil kills plankton and fish. It also coats the fur or feathers of marine mammals and birds. This destroys their protection from the cold, and many freeze to death.

Oil washes up on a Florida beach from the Deepwater Horizon oil spill disaster of 2010. Oil flowed nonstop for three months into the Gulf of Mexico from underwater pipes. It was the largest accidental marine oil spill in the history of the petroleum industry.

Although you may think of ocean pollution as garbage washed on shore, the majority of pollutants going into the ocean come from activities on land.

On April 20, 2010, an explosion at an oil-drilling platform in the Gulf of Mexico killed eleven people. It also broke underwater pipes that began leaking oil into the water. It took almost three months to stop the leak. By that time, more than 4 million barrels of oil had flowed into the ocean water. The oil killed thousands of animals and sea life. This huge oil spill may continue to damage ocean ecosystems for years to come.

Each year, millions of seabirds, sea turtles, fish, sharks, and marine mammals get tangled in marine debris or eat plastics that they have mistaken for food.

Overfishing

Many areas of the Atlantic are overfished. Waters are overfished when fish are caught there faster than they can reproduce.

One cause of overfishing is the use of enormous fishing nets called drift nets. Some are almost 30 miles (48 kilometers) long. All kinds of marine life get caught in these nets, but not all of them are wanted. Unwanted fish are called bycatch. Bycatch is thrown back into the ocean. Unfortunately, much of the returned bycatch will not survive.

Turtles are one common bycatch. Each year, four thousand turtles are killed by fishing nets in the waters off the southeastern United States.

Overuse is also destroying coral. Boats that move too close to coral damage it and the ecosystems it supports. About one fourth of the coral reefs around the world are already dead.

Endangered Species

Overfishing and pollution have led to the depletion of several marine species. A species is depleted when its population becomes very small.

Depletion of a species can lead to its extinction. When a species nears extinction, it is said to be endangered. Atlantic manatees, seals, turtles, and whales are all endangered.

Some countries have laws that protect endangered species. In addition, many countries have created marine sanctuaries. This is an area in the ocean where animals cannot be disturbed. There are several marine sanctuaries in the Atlantic.

All life on our planet depends on the well-being of our oceans and their ecosystems. Due to their delicate nature, oceans cannot withstand abuse for long, which is why the United Nations has created the Law of the Sea Treaty.

Law of the Sea Treaty

A group of countries called the United Nations (UN) is trying to help all of the oceans on Earth. They have written laws to protect the oceans. These laws are called the Law of the Sea Treaty. Many countries have agreed to follow the treaty.

    The Law of the Sea Treaty says that a country can control the water that lies within 200 miles (320 kilometers) of its coast. The rest of the ocean belongs to everyone. The treaty gives guidelines for how these open waters can be used.

    The Atlantic Ocean is a fascinating place. It holds resources that people have come to depend on. Most importantly, though, it is a vital part of the earth's ecosystem. Keeping the ocean healthy will help keep the earth healthy, so it is very important to take care of the Atlantic Ocean.

ATLANTIC OCEAN FACTS

Area: About 29,638,000 square miles (76,762,000 square kilometers)

Average Depth: 12,800 feet (3,926 meters)

Greatest Known Depth: The Puerto Rico Trench in the Caribbean Sea, 30,246 feet (9,219 meters)

Surface Temperature

Highest: About 86°F (30°C) near the equator

Lowest: About 28°F (−2°C) near where the Atlantic meets the Southern Ocean

Greatest Distance

North to South: About 10,900 miles (17,5402 kilometers)

East to West: About 5,500 miles (8,850 kilometers)

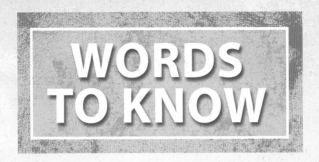

WORDS TO KNOW

abyssal plain—Any of the great flat areas of the ocean floor.

benthos—The area at the bottom of the ocean or other body of water; the plants and animals that live in this area.

bycatch—Any animals that are accidentally caught in fishing nets.

continental shelf—The submerged border of a large landmass.

coral—A polyp or a colony of polyps.

current—A strong movement of water in one direction.

ecosystem—All the plants and animals of a particular area that depend on one another for survival.

endangered—At risk of dying out completely.

hurricane—A strong, violent storm that occurs in the tropical areas of the Atlantic Ocean; it features winds of 74 miles (119 kilometers) per hour or greater, massive rainfall, thunder, and lightning.

invertebrate—An animal without a backbone.

latitude—An imaginary line around Earth that marks a distance north or south of the equator, measured in degrees.

longitude—An imaginary line around Earth that runs north to south and marks a distance east or west, measured in degrees.

lymphoma—A type of cancer that causes tumors to grow on the lymph nodes, which contain a bodily fluid important for survival.

mammal—Any of the warm-blooded animals that have a backbone, have fur or hair, and feed their offspring with mother's milk.

mid-ocean ridge—The underwater mountain range that runs through all the oceans of the world.

nekton—The group of the strong-swimming ocean animals that are not affected by waves and currents, such as whales, sharks, and squid.

ocean—The entire body of salt water that covers most of the earth, including the Atlantic Ocean, Pacific Ocean, Indian Ocean, Arctic Ocean, and Southern Ocean.

oceanographer—A scientist who studies the ocean.

Panama Canal—The waterway that was built across the country of Panama in Central America to connect the Atlantic and Pacific Oceans.

phytoplankton—Plant plankton.

plankton—Plants and animals, phytoplankton and zooplankton, that drift in the water.

pollution—Anything such as oil, garbage, and human waste that is not in its proper place.

polyp—A small animal that is shaped like a cylinder and has tentacles for drawing in food; many polyps live together to form coral.

Puerto Rico Trench—A long, very deep gash in the floor of the Atlantic Ocean at the border with the Caribbean Sea; the island of Puerto Rico lies close to this trench.

Strait of Gibraltar—The narrow channel of water between Spain and Africa that connects the Mediterranean Sea and the Atlantic Ocean.

tectonic plate—One of the thirty pieces of rock on which scientists believe Earth's surface rests. The movement of these plates causes earthquakes, volcanoes, and other changes to the surface.

tide—The regular rise or fall of sea level, caused by the Moon's pull on Earth's surface. There are usually two high tides and two low tides each day.

vertebrate—An animal that has a backbone, such as a mammal, bird, reptile, or fish.

water cycle—The series that Earth's water goes through, from clouds to rain or snow to rivers and oceans and then back again.

zooplankton—Animal plankton.

LEARN MORE

BOOKS

Benoit, Peter. *Oceans*. New York: Children's Press, 2011.

Jackson, Kay. *Explore the Ocean*. Mankato, Minn.: Capstone Press, 2007.

Jackson, Rebecca L. *Journey Into the Deep: Discovering New Ocean Creatures*. Minneapolis, Minn.: Millbrook Press, 2011.

Kalman, Bobbie. *Explore Earth's Five Oceans*. New York: Crabtree Publishing Company, 2010.

Ylvisaker Anne. *The Atlantic Ocean*. Mankato, Minn.: Capstone Press, 2006.

WEB SITES

Central Intelligence Agency. The World Factbook: *The Atlantic Ocean*. <https://www.cia.gov/library/publications/the-world-factbook/geos/zh.html>

NASA. *ClimateKids: NASA's Eyes on the Earth*. <http://climate.nasa.gov/kids/bigQuestions/oceanHappening/>

INDEX